SEEKING FREEDOM

THE UNTOLD STORY OF FORTRESS MONROE AND THE ENDING OF SLAVERY IN AMERICA

Selene Castrovilla

Illustrated by E. B. Lewis

CALKINS CREEK

AN IMPRINT OF ASTRA BOOKS FOR YOUNG READERS

New York

"I have no purpose, directly or indirectly,
to interfere with the institution
of slavery in the States where it exists.
I believe I have no lawful right to do so,
and I have no inclination to do so."

—President Abraham Lincoln's First Inaugural Address,
March 4, 1861

When President Abraham Lincoln took office on March 4, 1861, seven Southern states had left the United States. He prayed that his address would convince the remaining four Southern states to stay, but plantation owners, who depended on enslaved labor, didn't believe Lincoln. One by one, these states deserted to join the new Confederate States of America—waging war against their former country.

War broke out on April 12, 1861.

On April 17, 1861, Virginia abandoned the United States. When the enslaved people in Virginia heard the news, they knew that their families would be separated, the men dragged farther south and forced into hard labor: digging trenches, building fortifications, and hauling weapons to prepare for battle. They were desperate to prevent this. They would do anything to be free.

Throughout the book the word *Negro* is used for historical reasons. It was a term used in the nineteenth century and found in historical documentation. I have also used the original language of the Confiscation Acts and Emancipation Proclamation, nineteenth-century historical documents. Today *slave* and *fugitive* are considered dehumanizing—*enslaved* and *freedom seekers* are preferred.

MAY 26, 1861

GEORGE SCOTT hid behind a wide ash trunk, his cheek pressed against rough bark. The woods had been his home for two years, his bed the cold dirt of a dank cave. But it was far better than being tied to a whipping post.

Scott spent his days roaming the forest and swamp. He knew nearly every inch of them. But he *also* needed to know what was going on in the town of Hampton, and that was riskier. Hunters were in search of Negroes there. He *had* to prepare himself, to find out as much as he could, so that he'd be ready to move.

Negroes were in even higher demand because they were used for labor in the war effort. The mob after him would keep growing.

At the edge of a local farm, he overheard field hands whispering as they bent over crops, talking about three Negroes and how they had stolen a boat three nights since and rowed to the Union fortress nearby. How they hadn't been brought back.

Scott's heart lurched. *Could it be? Were the Union soldiers inside Fortress Monroe friends to Negroes?*

Steady now. His mind never raced.

He inched away in silence.

Through heavy thicket, Scott peered at the bridge to Fortress Monroe. He'd arrived to see eight more Negroes headed inside.

Hours later, there was still no sign of them! *Was it true? Were these people now among friends?*

MAY 27

Scott followed a large group of
Negroes across the bridge. They were
mostly barefoot, and many wore
clothing made of patches, all sewn
together. Scott frowned at the military
castoffs others wore—scraps of
Confederate uniforms snatched before
fleeing. Scott would rather be naked
than wear anything rebel. He slunk
back against a stone wall, last on the
long line to be interviewed.

MAJOR GENERAL BENJAMIN FRANKLIN BUTLER

felt exhausted—and frustrated. The commander of Fortress Monroe had spent precious hours behind his desk, questioning every Negro who had arrived, and hoping to get information about where Confederates were stationed—but receiving none.

How his life had changed in the few days since three freedom seekers appeared before him hoping for refuge and mercy. How his life had changed when a Confederate major turned up to take the three men back to their enslaver and Butler informed him: "I intend to hold them."

The major was stunned. How could Butler ignore his constitutional obligation to return the men? "I am under no constitutional obligations to a foreign country, which Virginia now claims to be," Butler replied. After all, he was a lawyer.

The major protested, but Butler silenced him. "I shall hold these Negroes as contraband of war." Contraband—property used for warlike purposes against the government of the United States—could be legally confiscated.

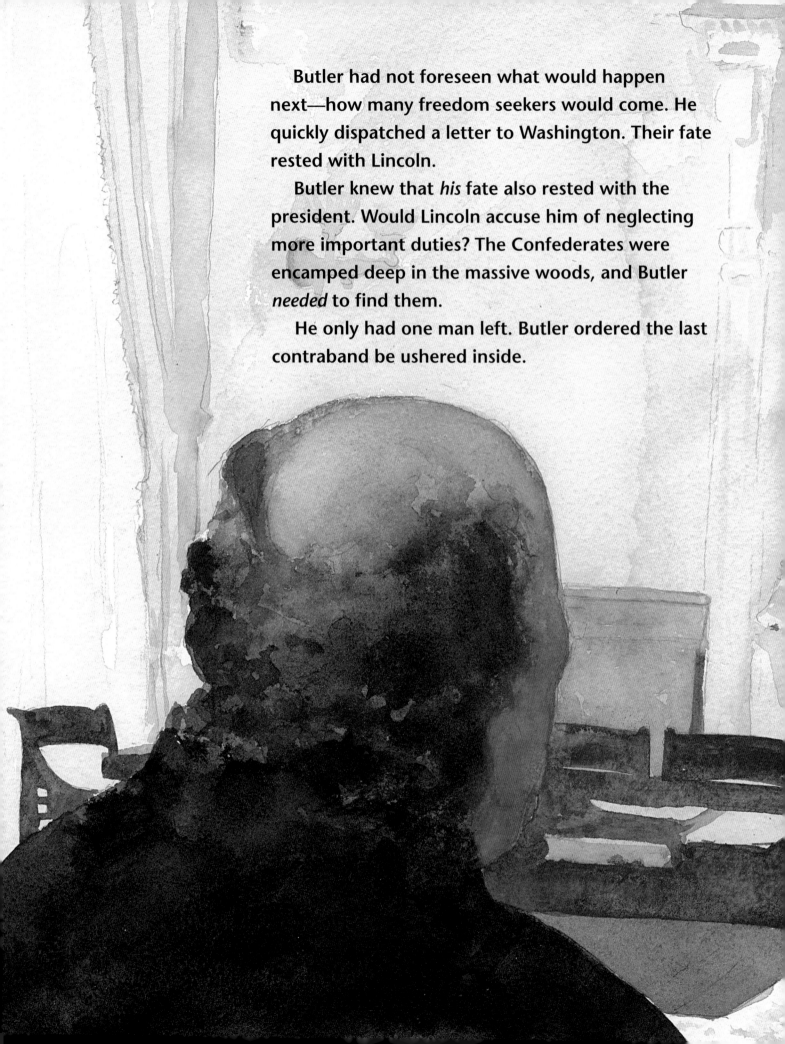

Butler had not foreseen what would happen next—how many freedom seekers would come. He quickly dispatched a letter to Washington. Their fate rested with Lincoln.

Butler knew that *his* fate also rested with the president. Would Lincoln accuse him of neglecting more important duties? The Confederates were encamped deep in the massive woods, and Butler *needed* to find them.

He only had one man left. Butler ordered the last contraband be ushered inside.

Scott told Butler he had seen many Confederates skulking around in the woods, and he had an idea about the direction they were headed.

Butler smiled. He had a mission for George Scott—to track down the Confederates.

EARLY JUNE

Scott maneuvered around trees and rough terrain. He'd trek all night if he had to.

News from Washington! Butler's hand shook as he read the letter: "SIR: Your action in respect to the negroes who came within your lines from the service of the rebels is approved."

Glorious words! But would the fortress remain secure against enemy attack? Butler's prayers were with Scott.

Scott trekked for eight dense, rocky miles.

He *had* to be close. Could he have veered wrong?

Daybreak. Scott was weary, with no rebels in sight. He looked at the sky: *Dear Lord, please lead the way!*

Just then a noise. Scott glimpsed a Confederate-uniformed figure yards ahead. Scott shadowed him—to discover thousands of Confederates outside a church. *His* prayers had been answered.

Scott sank behind a bush and listened.

All day. *Stay still!* All night. *Remember!*

Then, the unthinkable! A Confederate sentry spotted him and cried out.

Scott bolted, kicking up dirt and rocks. Catapulting through gunfire. A bullet grazed his sleeve as he raced back toward the fortress with the news—the rebels were preparing to cut off all supplies.

Scott helped Butler draw a plan of attack. It needed to be executed—quick!

JUNE 10, MIDNIGHT

Armed with a revolver, Scott rode off near the front of an infantry of five thousand men. This time, he was sure of the way. But would the Confederates be gone?

Scott and the infantry sighted the church. Yes, the enemy was still there! They raised their guns to fire . . . but shots blasted at them first!

An ambush, from all directions! Word had leaked to the Confederates.

Chaos came fast. The loss . . . tremendous.

MID-JUNE

Butler's men had not died in vain. The Confederates had fled; the threat to the fortress was over. But how could Butler reward Scott? When Scott asked for freedom, Butler put his legal skills to work.

Butler began his letter to President Lincoln arguing for Scott's liberty—and for that of all the contrabands.

Hampton was empty and destroyed, as were other nearby towns. These contrabands had been property, but since they had been abandoned, they were now simply men, women, and children.

Butler implored the President and Congress:

These human beings must be given the free enjoyment of life, liberty, and the pursuit of happiness.

With Butler's letter as legal ammunition, Scott journeyed to the capital to ask for his freedom. It wasn't long before Butler's words took effect. Congress passed an act approving the confiscation of fugitive slaves by the federal government—and freeing all people enslaved by the Confederacy. President Abraham Lincoln signed it into law, sparking the end of slavery in America.

AFTERMATH

Benjamin Butler was relieved from his command at Fortress Monroe after he wrote Scott's letter. His superiors did not appreciate Butler's outspokenness. But the contrabands remained. Thousands found refuge there.

Butler's landmark action received the nation's attention, fueling the movement for emancipation. This pressure pushed the government, which had not wanted to address the slavery issue, to create The Confiscation Act of 1861. Signed into law on August 6, this act authorized the Union seizure of rebel property, and stated that all "persons" who fought with or worked for the Confederate military services were freed of further obligations to their "owners."

The Confiscation Act of 1862, signed into law on July 17, went further—stating that any person committing treason against the United States would have their "slaves" liberated in criminal proceedings. Confederates were given sixty days to surrender and pledge their loyalty to the Union. This could only be enforced if the Confederates were captured.

On September 22, 1862, Lincoln warned that he would order the emancipation of all "slaves" in any state that did not end its rebellion against the Union by January 1, 1863.

President Lincoln issued the Emancipation Proclamation on January 1, 1863, changing the status of three million people enslaved by Confederates from "slave" to "free." But this was a murky law for the contrabands, who were no longer "slaves," but confiscated property, at the time of the proclamation. It also did not cover "slaves" in Union states.

The Thirteenth Amendment to the United States Constitution banished slavery everywhere in America when it was ratified on December 6, 1865.

LC-B8171-2594

The War For the Union. 1865

1861

1861 Photographic War History. 1865

2594. A Group of "Contrabands."
[FOR DESCRIPTION OF THIS VIEW SEE THE OTHER SIDE OF THIS CARD.]

Group of Virginia contrabands wearing old Civil War uniforms

THE CONTRABANDS

Three pioneers named Frank Baker, Shepard Mallory, and James Townsend led the way for thousands of refugees, all seeking emancipation. "There is a universal desire among the slaves to be free," wrote Edward L. Pierce, who served as Commissioner of Negro Affairs at Fortress Monroe. "When we said to them, 'You don't want to be free—your masters say you don't,'—they manifested much indignation, answering, 'We do want to be free,—we want to be for ourselves.' . . . Even old men and women, with crooked backs, who could hardly walk or see, shared the same feeling."

As the number of contrabands increased, Fortress Monroe could no longer house them all, so they built their own camp on the other side of the moat, in the burned ruins of Hampton. Their new home was called Grand Contraband Camp—which they nicknamed "Slabtown."

"There was a very general desire among the contrabands to know how to read," wrote Pierce. Contraband children were the earliest formerly enslaved African Americans to receive education in America. Mary Smith Peake taught the first classes on September 17, 1861.

The contrabands contributed to the Union war efforts by digging entrenchments and building weapons stations. Pierce reported, "The contrabands worked well, and in no instance was it found necessary for the superintendents to urge them." He called them "honest hearts" and felt that they deserved freedom as much as he did.

People came from all over the Union to meet the contrabands, and reporters regularly wrote articles about them. One visitor commented, "I think everyone likes them." A *New York Times* reporter observed the contrabands marching to work: "Their shovels and their other implements of labor, they handle and carry as soldiers do their guns . . . they do not straggle . . . but fall into regular files and columns, and with a step and regularity that would do credit to enlisted men, march with clearly defined pride . . . I have no doubt they would make fair or even excellent soldiers."

These refugees raised Northern awareness with their tales of torture and loss at the hands of their vicious enslavers. No longer could Northerners deny that slavery was abominable, or that Negroes were just like them in every way except for the color of their skin. They were human beings, deserving of dignity, respect, and liberty. Lydia Maria Child, a northerner who fought for emancipation, wrote, "Where we are drifting, I cannot see, but we are drifting somewhere, and our fate . . . is bound up with these . . . 'contrabands.'"

Contraband camps spread throughout Union-controlled areas of the South, and there were one hundred by the end of the war.

These refugees served the Union faithfully and diligently, and asked for their freedom in exchange.

"And will the Government be so false as ever to fail to protect every Negro who has ever served our officers or men, helped to build our defences, or in any way aided our cause? If it shall ever be so base and treacherous as that, it will deserve to be a thousand times overthrown, and be forever accursed among the nations."
—Edward L. Pierce

Contraband men, women, and children in Virginia

BENJAMIN BUTLER'S LEGACY

"I think we can no longer dispense with Gen. Butler's services."

—Abraham Lincoln

Benjamin Butler almost left the army after his dismissal from Fortress Monroe. He decided to stay when his superiors asked him to travel down south on a vital mission: capturing New Orleans.

Before Butler left, Lincoln asked Butler to avoid raising problems or controversies. Butler respected Lincoln's wishes when he took command of the conquered New Orleans, but he did continue trying to improve Negro lives.

Butler's policy of claiming freedom seekers as contraband was famous. Thousands of Negroes in Louisiana flocked to the army, seeking refuge. Butler established colonies of freedom seekers to work on confiscated or abandoned plantations. He also arranged a labor contract for the Negroes.

Butler created the 1st Louisiana Native Guard—one of the earliest Union brigades of African American soldiers in the United States. After that, Butler organized a larger Negro brigade, with three regiments and artillery. He said of them, "Better soldiers never shouldered a musket."

After Butler ordered the execution of a Confederate who murdered a Negro, the rebels called him "Beast Butler," and cartoons of him as a beast were featured on flyers and in the newspapers.

Butler returned to command at Fortress Monroe in November 1863. He increased the pay for Negroes enlisted in the army under his command, and asked the government to do so for all Negroes.

That same year, Butler founded the Butler School for Negro Children in Hampton, Virginia, to continue the work of Mary Smith Peake, who passed away in 1862. Butler also bought farms confiscated from Confederates and turned them over to African Americans.

Throughout his military career, Butler met with much opposition due to his headstrong personality, but Abraham Lincoln held him in the highest esteem. When Butler considered ending his service, Lincoln urged him to stay. After the war Lincoln called on Butler again, to discuss how America could best integrate formerly enslaved people into society. Before anything could be decided, Lincoln was assassinated.

Butler entered politics in Massachusetts, his home state. He was elected to the US House of Representatives. He wrote the original version of the Ku Klux Klan Act of 1871, empowering President Ulysses S. Grant to fight the Ku Klux Klan and other white supremacy groups. This landmark statute continues to be important in courts, and is still used to fight discrimination.

Butler also cosponsored the Civil Rights Act of 1875, "to protect all citizens in their civil and legal rights." This law was not popular with the public. In 1883, the Supreme Court declared parts of the act unconstitutional and struck it down. This was the last civil rights bill to be signed into law until the passage of the Civil Rights Act of 1957.

Major General Benjamin Franklin Butler

In 1882, Butler was elected governor of Massachusetts. He appointed the state's first African American judge, as well as its first Irish American one. He also appointed the first woman to executive office.

What began with an ingenious twist on the law grew into a lifetime of devotion to civil rights—Benjamin Butler's legacy.

GEORGE SCOTT

Born into slavery near Hampton, Virginia, George Scott was sold to a brutal man named A. M. Graves. But before Graves could claim him, Scott ran away into the woods. He hid there for two years. The enraged Graves found and cornered him, but Scott fought Graves off and disarmed him.

One of the first contrabands, Scott volunteered to track down the Confederates. He promised "I ken smell a rebel furderer dan I ken a skunk," and he kept his word.

He was the first African American to be armed during the Civil War.

It is not known if Scott achieved his goal of asking President Lincoln for his freedom.

There is no known image of George Scott. William Headly (shown here) shared a similar story to Scott. Headly escaped enslavement, surviving six weeks of persecution to become a contraband in North Carolina. His cloak is an old cotton grain bag.

VISIT FORT MONROE HAMPTON, VIRGINIA

Fort Monroe, formerly called Fortress Monroe, the largest stone fort in America, is no longer an active military base and it is open to the public. Quarters 1, where General Butler met the three freedom seekers, still stands. On a separate occasion, President Abraham Lincoln stayed there.

Ironically, Robert E. Lee, the commanding general of the Confederate army, also had quarters at Fort Monroe. That's because long before the Civil War, when he was a young US Army officer, he was stationed there—and he played an important role in planning the fort's impenetrable design.

President Barack Obama proclaimed Fort Monroe to be a national monument in 2011 (see next spread).

There is a museum at Fort Monroe, in the small rooms built within the fortress's thick walls. These rooms are called casemates. The Casemate Museum gives a vivid military history of the fort. It explains much about the contrabands and General Butler, and offers many other interesting facts. For example, author Edgar Allan Poe was stationed there during his brief military career.

When the war ended, Confederate President Jefferson Davis was arrested and imprisoned at Fort Monroe. You can visit the casemate he lived in, and see the actual US flag he was forced to look at—a reminder that the Confederacy had been defeated.

FORTRESS MONROE, VA. AND ITS VICINITY.

1. Old Point Comfort	5. Rip Raps	9. Elizabeth River	13. Atlantic Ocean	17. Newport News
2. Fortress Monroe	6. Chesapeake Bay	10. Norfolk	14. Cape Hatteras, N C	18. Hampton
3. Water Battery	7. Sewall's Point	11. Portsmouth	15. Nansemond River	19. Mill Creek
4. Hampton Roads	8. Craney Island	12. Dismal Swamp	16. James River	20. Land approach to Fortress

An 1862 print of Fortress Monroe

BIBLIOGRAPHY

All quotations used in the book can be found in the following sources marked with an asterisk (*).

*Butler, Benjamin F. *Benjamin F. Butler Papers, 1778–1929*. Library of Congress Manuscript Division, Washington, DC.

*——. *Butler's Book: Autobiography and Personal Reminiscences of Maj-Gen Benjamin F. Butler*. Boston: A. M. Thayer & Co., 1892.

*——. *Private and Official Correspondence of Gen. Benjamin F. Butler, during the Period of the Civil War*. Compiled by Jessie Ames Marshall. Norwood, MA: Plimpton Press, 1917.

Cobb, J. Michael. "Rehearsing Reconstruction in Occupied Virginia: Life and Emancipation at Fort Monroe," in *Virginia at War, 1861*. Edited by William C. David and James I. Robertson Jr. Lexington, KY: University Press of Kentucky, 2005.

Engs, Robert Francis. *Freedom's First Generation: Black Hampton, Virginia, 1861–1890*. Philadelphia: University of Pennsylvania Press, 1979.

Foner, Eric. *The Fiery Trial: Abraham Lincoln and American Slavery*. New York: W. W. Norton, 2010.

Goodheart, Adam. *1861: The Civil War Awakening*. New York: Alfred A. Knopf, 2011.

Lockwood, Lewis C. to Dear Brethren, March 26, 1862 and April 17, 1862. American Missionary Association Papers, Tulane University.

Nash, Howard P., Jr. *Stormy Petrel: The Life and Times of General Benjamin Butler, 1818–1893*. Rutherford, NJ: Fairleigh Dickinson University Press, 1969.

Nolan, Dick. *Benjamin Franklin Butler: The Damnedest Yankee*. Novato, CA: Presidio Press, 1991.

*Pierce, Edward Lillie. "The Contrabands at Fortress Monroe." *Atlantic Monthly*, November 1861.

*Poland, Charles P., Jr. *The Glories of War: Small Battles and Early Heroes of 1861*. Bloomington, IN: AuthorHouse, 2004.

Nicolay, John G., and John Hay. *Abraham Lincoln: A History*. New York: The Century Co., 1890.

West, Richard S. *Lincoln's Scapegoat General: A Life of Benjamin F. Butler*. Boston: Houghton Mifflin Company, 1965.

Winthrop, Theodore. *The Life and Poems of Theodore Winthrop*. New York: Henry Holt and Company, 1884.

NEWSPAPERS & MAGAZINES (IN 1861):
Atlantic Monthly
Boston Traveller
Frank Leslie's Illustrated Newspaper
The Independent
New York Herald
**New York Times*
New-York Tribune
New York World
Philadelphia Inquirer
Springfield Republican
Trenton Daily State Gazette and Republican
Weekly Anglo-African

ACKNOWLEDGMENTS

Thank you to my fellow American Friends of Lafayette, who arranged the day trip to Fort Monroe, which began my journey toward this book. Particular gratitude to Bonnie Fritz, who insisted that I would "find my next story" at the fort.

I cannot stress how passionate and thorough former Fort Monroe Casemate Museum historian Robert Kelly was in his research. I am grateful that he passed that fervor to me.

Thank you to the Bank Street Writers Lab at Bank Street College of Education, who provided me with their thoughts and feedback on this book.

PICTURE CREDITS

ESTABLISHMENT OF THE FORT MONROE NATIONAL MONUMENT:
BY THE PRESIDENT OF THE UNITED STATES OF AMERICA

A PROCLAMATION

From left: Adam Goodheart, Civil War historian, Washington College; Rep. Scott Rigell, R-VA.; Rep. Bobby Scott, D-VA.; Mayor Molly Ward, Hampton, VA.; Interior Secretary Ken Salazar; Sen. Mark Warner, D-VA.; Lacy Ward Jr., director, Robert Russa Moton Museum, Farmville, VA.; and Rep. Emanuel Cleaver, D-MO.; observe President Barack Obama sign the Proclamation.

Known first as "The Gibraltar of the Chesapeake" and later as "Freedom's Fortress," Fort Monroe on Old Point Comfort in Virginia has a storied history in the defense of our Nation and the struggle for freedom.

Fort Monroe, designed by Simon Bernard and built of stone and brick between 1819 and 1834 in part by enslaved labor, is the largest of the Third System of fortifications in the United States. It has been a bastion of

defense of the Chesapeake Bay, a stronghold of the Union Army surrounded by the Confederacy, a place of freedom for the enslaved, and the imprisonment site of Chief Blackhawk and the President of the Confederacy, Jefferson Davis. It served as the U.S. Army's Coastal Defense Artillery School during the 19th and 20th centuries, and most recently, as headquarters of the U.S. Army's Training and Doctrine Command.

Old Point Comfort in present day Hampton, Virginia, was originally named "Pointe Comfort" by Captain John Smith in 1607 when the first English colonists came to America. . . . The first enslaved Africans in England's colonies in America were brought to this peninsula on a ship flying the Dutch flag in 1619, beginning a long ignoble period of slavery in the colonies and, later, this Nation. Two hundred and forty-two years later, Fort Monroe became a place of refuge for those later generations escaping enslavement.

During the Civil War, Fort Monroe stood as a foremost Union outpost in the midst of the Confederacy and remained under Union Army control during the entire conflict. The Fort was the site of General Benjamin Butler's "Contraband Decision" in 1861, which provided a pathway to freedom for thousands of enslaved people during the Civil War and served as a forerunner of President Abraham Lincoln's Emancipation Proclamation of 1863. Thus, Old Point Comfort marks both the beginning and end of slavery in our Nation. . . .

—Barack Obama, November 1, 2011

To Robert Kelly, former Casemate
Museum historian at Fort Monroe, who
told me about Major General Butler's
contraband decision —SC

To all the freedom seekers worldwide and
their contributions to change —EBL

Calkins Creek
An imprint of Astra Books for Young Readers,
a division of Astra Publishing House
calkinscreekbooks.com

Printed in China

ISBN: 978-1-63592-582-1 (hc)
ISBN: 978-1-63592-564-7 (eBook)
Library of Congress Control Number: 2021906403

First edition
10 9 8 7 6 5 4 3 2 1

Design by Barbara Grzeslo
The text is set in Stone Sans ITC Std.
The titles are set in ITC Machine Std Medium.
The illustrations are exclusively done in watercolor.